Of Rowan and Pearl

Of Rowan and Pearl

poems of rural Scotland

Margaret Gillies Brown
&
Kenneth C Steven

Argyll
publishing

© Margaret Gillies Brown &
Kenneth C Steven 2000

First published 2000
Argyll Publishing
Glendaruel
Argyll PA22 3AE
Scotland
www.deliberatelythirsty.com

The authors have asserted their
moral rights.

British Library Cataloguing-in-Publication Data.
A catalogue record for this
book is available from the
British Library.

ISBN 1 902831 23 3

Illustrations
Susan Gillies

Cover Photo
Campbell R Steven

Printing
ColourBooks Ltd, Dublin

Poems in Margaret Gillies
Brown's collection previously
appeared in:
Outposts Publications, Akros
Publications, Blind Serpent,
Poetry Scotland, Poetry Monthly,
Life and Work, The Fireside
Book, Ver Poets Freda Downie
Anthology, Envoi, Poetry
Nottingham International, and
New Hope International.

Poems in Kenneth Steven's
collection were first published in:
Edinburgh Review, Gairfish,
Envoi, Poetry Wales, The Scots
Magazine, Orbis, Month, New
Quarterly (Canada), Poetry
Nineties Review, New Writer,
Poetry Scotland, Other Poetry,
Imago (Australia), Planet and
The Yorkshire Journal.

Contents

Fishing for Pearls
Kenneth C Steven

Foreword

THOSE of us who love poetry treasure our favourite poems and they become a priceless part of our heritage.

Some appeal by virtue of their subject matter – a particular area which is dear to our hearts, or the ever-changing beauty of the countryside, nostalgia for a lost childhood or the varied idiosyncrasies of some of the people we have known.

Or sometimes it is the craftsmanship of the poem that appeals – the aptness and ex citement of the sound of the words, a stunning rhythm, a startling image, a poetic vision – because we have experienced exactly the same feelings as the poet.

The poems in this book contain much to delight the reader. Anyone who loves Scotland will feel instantly at home, with the evocative use of language that conjures up its seas and mountains, its wildlife and its doughty characters. There are lines to savour and moments to share in a celebration of the diversity of human life in familiar experiences.

The craftsmanship displayed in the poems is impressive. A glance at the acknowledgements showing the string of publications where some have previously appeared in print will confirm that I am not the only supporter of this view. Each poet tackles her/his task with a sure technique. My favourite images? Margaret's 'owl on woollen wing' and the durability of her 'Village Woman' who 'lives in the echo of the hills'. And Kenneth's wasps who 'invaded like a gang of bikers/ in their yellow and black jackets, and the snow that 'came petalling from the skies,/ Settled into a deep quilt. . .' I found many more.

There is much to compare in both these poets, for both collections are imbued with the spirit of Scotland and its countryside. But as a contrast we have differing points of view from the perspective of age. Margaret's poems are the result of a lifetime of experience and the wisdom of maturity, and Kenneth's are full of the adventure of being (comparatively) young. It is this balance and both poets' observations that have given me so much delight. This book will be an inspiration and a lasting joy for all its readers.

Jean Sergeant
September 2000

The Green Rowan Tree

Margaret Gillies Brown

Dedicated to James Hall Thomson and the Saggar Poets

Rumbling Brig

No moderation here –

A force of water falls
tremendously! Tons of it
shoot down sheer rock
and peat-brown tongues spume out
become white flounces
that hurtle into foam vivid as soap suds
on the black unfathomed pool.

Cross the bridge,
peer over parapet –
Calmer here,
water moves darkly on.
Almost autumn –
Up the steep banks
colours today are muted,
grey rock, grey trunk, grey lichen,
green merging into green
with just a hint of yellow
but the rowan –
Look at the rowan
Its wrinkling ferny leaves
cannot calm these berries
that flare out in bunches
enamelled in sheerest red. . .

No moderation here!

Disused Saw Mill

Deserted now, this building made of stone,
Its facade crumbling, pantiles overgrown,
Green mosses mingling with the fading red;
Lonely, the lark sings somewhere overhead
And from the threshold steps a straying sheep,
Around a lichened rock the windflowers creep.

A stillness has descended on this place,
Vigour that once was here has left small trace,
No sound of man, the burn slides dankly on,
The song of timber, smell of wood-dust – gone!
Higher, the dam is now a tree dimmed lake.
Feathered and fish-ringed, only half awake.

Silent, a statue hints at what is past
Fashioned from stone to weather winter's blast
By one who loved man, glorious of limb,
And chiselled well an effigy to him,
Aware, perhaps, one day this place would die,
That he must leave this symbol on the sky.

Road to Rannoch

Take the road
From Coshieville to Rannoch,
Schiehallion under cloud – in autumn,
Take wilderness and water,
Narrow winding from nowhere to nowhere.

Take colour, colour, colour,
Deepened by wet,
Rich breathing tapestry:
Artist take blending,
Match it if you can –
Bracken-brown to yellow fern tip
Springing on leaves, shading to gold, orange, red
And its pure essence in rowans hanging earthward,
Miss a beat of colour – jump
To lacquer-black in elderberries.

Take pattern imposed on pattern,
Leaf shape on branch,
Branch-angle on trees
Trees against a rising patchwork
To where high-hill-ridges
Are irregular moving shapes
Against flying ragged grey.

Take contrast intricate as the universe;
Bright-limned against dark
Yet always making a whole
No falseness anywhere;

See those distant sheep,
Pale as river pearls!
Look up at the dark, dying heather
Marked by streaking silver
Like an ageing woman's hair.

Lower, black peat pools
Hide in tawny reeds
And grey sheets of water
Watch cushions of moss,
Sphagnum-green as elf-light.
Under the trees the forest carpet
Takes the colour of pheasant's wings.

The cloud is broken,
from the gold pocket
a shaft of sunlight drops –
Glory, glory, glory . . .

I'm thrown above Schiehallion.

Glenfargie Hill

The ear no longer hears the summer fiddler in the grass,
The bat-pitched radar voices in the moonlight;
The eye no longer sees faint blush on windflower,
The satin glow on celandine;
Quince is less bitter to the tongue,
Honey less sweet, the delicate scent
Of primrose has to be helped by memory.

But spirit has no age . . .

We who sought and found
Stumbling past the milestones on the way,

Knocked and were admitted, embraced the paradox –
Have come through hoops of fire –
Know the importance of now.

And now is ourselves, here on the crowning top
Of this green hill in April –
Pilgrims perceiving from a high place
The far mountains still streaked with snow,
Fertile valleys, huddled villages along the shining river
And in the distance the smokeless high rise city.
Under our well shod feet this vivid grass,
Over bare heads –
Blue the colour of infinite distance.

Lambs bask in sunlight while their dams rake the hillside
And the in-calf heifers beside the hay hake
Gleam black and white
Too heavy and content to be curious.
A lapwing, crazy with joy, clowns earthward,
A curlew calls, planes to its chosen tussock,
Buzzards above their windy Kingdom,
Wheel in lazy circles ready to plunge on smallest move
Seen through the telescopic facets of fierce eyes.

We ramble over green swards
Forgetting yesterday and tomorrow
Knowing that now is the time for celebration.

Winter Evening

In mellow notes
The church tower clock
Strikes seven;
The suppered village stirs.
Savoury smells
Of frying fish
Seep under the door
Of the corner shop
And herald its opening.
Opposite, under the dim lights
That keep the dark at bay,
A gang of boys and bikes
Gather and discuss
Football, girls, the insides of engines,
Take sudden bursts of energy
And boast on brumming bikes
Up, round the cross and down again
Or breenge across the road
To where Chippie Jean
Dispenses discipline, chips and sound advice
In equal portions.
Lassies saunter up in twos
To lean shoulders against
The cold Co-op wall
Legs out and near enough
To have their saucy sallies
Slung at the boys
Boomerang back.
Youth stands here on the kerb of life

Waiting;
The girls with patient eyes
For 'Goodbye Joe – halloo Josephine',
The boys for their eighteenth year
And walking through the portals
Into the pub and manhood.

At a safe distance
From big brothers,
Smaller laddies
Play at torchy;
Up black alleys,
In the shadows,
With springing step on legs
That still would rather run than walk,
Transmit excitement,
Electrify the air
With the mysteries
Of childhood and night
Until, from the meeting hut,
A giggle of brownies
On dancing feet
Quickly trip
To the safety of the nest.

The clock strikes ten
And closing time.
From the warm laughter
Of the snug and smoky bar
Old Ted topples,
For a moment
He and the wall collide
And then
On his brave recovery
Weaves widely home
To waiting tight-lipped Morag.
Next dark-haired Don

Steps out
Whistling a cheerful tune;
Right now for him it seems
The World's a glorious place,
The night's his oyster
As he makes with confident gait
For some unsuspecting sonsie Meg.
The half-closed door spits out the rest
In threes, in twos, in ones.
The cop car flashing red and white
Passes, flaunts up and round and down
But doesn't stop.

Rumblings erupt from the village hall;
Rural over for another week.
A chatter of women bunch out
And stand in small groups
Talking of
Poor Mrs Speedy,
Jane's hacking cough,
The wee one's grumbling teeth,
The scandalous price of butter,
Until
Icy fingers of frost
Cut through coats
And they hurry towards
Warm promise
Of their own firesides.

Soon only the yowling cat
Prowls the empty night
And the houses huddle
As the east wind
Snell and keen
Sweeps down the village street
And brushes it clean for tomorrow.

Mistress of the Village Shop

SIMPSON –
Large letters bold-white on red!
And squatting underneath –
The tiny shop;
This is your life;
A low door opens
With singing-ping of bell
To Sunshine –
We find you bustling from back room
to serve with smiles,
Those you count less customers than friends,
Apologising always for the price of goods
We find cheapest here.
'Draper' perhaps you call yourself,
A narrow term to cover all that's carried,
Aspirins and ornaments, clothes and kirby grips,
Wool and willow pattern – you WANT it –
Mrs Simpson HAS it!
With cheerfulness thrown in as bonus.

Children find in this place, a nucleus,
Toys, books, novelties, inexpensive geegaws;
Here they can change hot pennies
For some heart's desire:
With them you stray into Aladdin's cave;
Engrossed in helping in a tricky choice,
Become again, a child.

Morning sees the burdened Mother
Climb the weary street –
And on the way to Doctor's surgery
Pop in your door, tell you her troubles,
Listens to the practical advice,
Talk, tales and tonic laughter,
Finds this medicine enough.
And sometimes gets no further.

The Village Doctor

He tended his flock
After his own fashion,
Unorthodox at times
Lancet might not have understood
His language
But we
The people of the village
Knew just what he meant,
Talking to us with robust and country vigour
Telling the men among us
Many a ribald tale,
Speaking of sport
Rather than ailments.

Children went to him
Like bees to certain honey,
Sometimes feigning illness
When they thought him to be near;
He knew our fears and foibles,
Our problems,
Cured us when he could,
Jollied us through jungles of despair,
Laughed with us, cried with us
He loved us
Though he never would have said so,
Poo-poohed all praise
And turned away from it.

Old folk were never left
To feel alone,
Getting unscheduled visits
To cheer their winter's day,
Make sure they needed nothing.
Road accidents he hated
Till it showed.

Once
Rocked in his strong arms
The mutilated body of a child
Till help came
Crooning
As tenderly as any Mother
Poor wee lamb,
My poor wee lamb.
Felt with a sixth sense
For the feelings
Of a woman in childbirth
And her emerging babe;
Showed unexpected gentleness,
Sighed with satisfaction
At the new cot-cuddled bairn
Stating all best babies
Born at home.

Life never lost for him its fascination
Nor he his deep compassion.

The Blacksmith

Stocky and strong,
Tender yet tough,
Red-haired, red-bearded
Blacksmith.
One who knew all the passions
Centigrades higher
Than other men,
Yet horses felt
His gentle compassion.
Knew him their friend,
'Whoa there, lass!'

Gone . . .
This amalgam of men,
Fired by fire-water,
Beaten out boldly
On a ring-dinging anvil,
Sad player of Pibrochs,
Glad Gaelic bard,
Artistic Celt
Bending straight metal
Into curved wrought-iron scrolls,
Pulpit thumping lay preacher,
('Beware the red woman')
Laughter's bright centre
At midnight's loud ceilidh,
Great lover of life.

Gone . . .
With pain's white hot sizzle,
Angina's forked lightning –

All his elements earthed.

Village Woman
For Mrs Hodge

It's her durability that astounds.
She lives in the echo of hills,
Near run of the pearled river
In a folk-weave village
Skelped by the wind.

She is –
Child bearer,
Housekeeper,
Hen husbander,
Potato picker –
Born to bend into strong breezes.

Now at seventy –
Grandmother,
Great grandmother,
She feels loss if the storm lessens . . .

Looks for more gale
To fight against.

Susie's Washing

The rainbow's over Windyrigg today
Susie's washing's blowing on the line
And all the men for miles around
In farms and lonely cottages,
Turn smouldering thoughts
To curves and come-on glances,
A dark-haired siren singing on the hill.

Some, tempting fate, nibble at the bait
While country dames denounce her!

Sheba

Sheba is quite different,
Outrageous some would say,
She comes in richest greens and golds
to light the dullest day
And make us wonder, yet again,
At our banality.

Sheba is quite different:
she loves to shock the staid
And show us where a southern sun
Has on her body played
till men's thoughts turn to amour
And women – are afraid!

We only meet at parties
With sometimes years between
Where always there is laughter
And always Sheba's queen.
But where in all these lost years –
Where has Sheba been? . . .

And when at night she waits for sleep
I wonder, does she ever weep?

Dundee from a Distance

City standing on the skyline
I often gaze at you across the coloured carse;
The quality of light chooses for me
The way I feel about you.

In days of sun and shade
You are intriguing;
Bright, high-rise sentinels
Drawn against the sky
Guard
The maze of houses
Making me think of somewhere
In some Southern land
That beckons
Until I want to leave these empty fields,
Explore
Your curves and corners
Your varied architecture,
Fascinating world of men.

On cloud-filled days
Diverse varieties of dullness
Lose many buildings in the landscape;
The concrete geometry that remains
Appears mundane,
Uninteresting,
Does not stir imagination
One degree.

In yet more sombre hours
Square towers
Become stark obelisks
Against a lowering lift,
Prophesying doom.

But there are moments
When thoughts of you
Enter a new dimension
As some spectacular sun
Descends in glory
Behind the Sidlaw hills,
By natural tricks
Of light and white mist
You appear
Elevated above this common earth,
A shining, a celestial city:
A multitude of windows
reflect the blazing splendour,
The eternal fire
And as the mirage fades
Beyond the shadowed valley
The soul stretches out to reach it,
Yearning.

Legend

Centuries ago a French trading ship was wrecked on the treacherous rocks off the east Aberdeenshire coast. Miraculously, the captain's twin baby sons were saved, along with the ship's log. The boys were brought up by local fisher folk and married into the community.

My Mother lived a legend.
Dark-haired, vivacious,
Vivid as November's morning star,
She claimed to be a hark-back
To the French – (the other half
Of that 'Auld Alliance')
To one of the twins snatched from the roaring seas.
She did much to make this myth come true:
Brought foreign thought to young parochial minds,
Inspired us with French stories.

Her imagination lit our lives.
Our garden, dull at the back,
Plain grass, grey walls
And spindly trees, thin in their moving shadow,
Became for us a cool French courtyard,
Giving it charm and mystery
Where it had none.

She travelled once to France before our birth,
Told us of feeling at home
The moment foot touched land
And talked of places,

Strange marbling to the tongue,
Versailles and Sacre Coeur.

Once we saw her weep –
The day France fell
And for a while
Light vanished from the courtyard,
Yet after the first strong shock
Her faith returned –
'One day!' she said, 'One day . . .'

Wars fought and won,
She never made for France
(No money and no time
Were her excuses).
Looking back it seems,
For her, dreams were enough –
Wishing was the mother of invention,
Believing was becoming.

Boundaries

Mother surrounded us with fences,
tight strands of dos and donts,
rights and wrongs for our own safety:
High tensile, shot through with love.

Even after they were gone, ripped out,
we didn't seek to stray
or if we did, like sheep bonded to a hillside,
soon found the green way back.

She is no longer earth
but still the boundaries of her love remain.

Ancestors

. . . And here we are again in this strange land
To feel the pull in sinews, blood and bones,
This walled-in graveyard swept by ocean winds
Where farmers lie with fishers from St Combs,
Here, where all strife ends, I read the names engraved
And marvel at the height and strength of tombs,
Our ancestors, the far flung empires of their days,
Reach out and touch us in surprising ways.

This sea, this sky, this landscape that they knew
Better than the back of weathered hand,
This salty, windswept ever stubborn land
Touches lost chords where shelter belts of trees
Are stunted, grotesque shadows. Here we stand
And see the amazing crops beyond the wall
Where old lost voices of smeddum call.

Today a sky sculptured in shades of grey
Shows the odd chink of azure-giving grace,
We twist along the narrow, winding roads
Running like lines upon an ageing woman's face
To reach a solid house defiant to all storms
Here roses in profusion give no trace
Of hardship, only the country welcome that we get
Talks of yesterday where common ancestors met.

Most things must change within unyielding time;
Where once the clod was turned with little gain,
And daily used the girdle, cheesepress, churn

Now this wild place of fish and fowl and grain
Has taken in its stride the better ways
Today's machinery removes the strains
and peatmoss benefits from running drains.

But still wild seas, cold winds,
The grotesque trees remain.

The Grandfather Clock

In my Aunt's farmhouse, tick tock, tick tock
The pendulum swung in the old brown clock,
How gold-note-calm and distinct each chime
Up the steep stairway deigned to climb.
Still half-asleep I counted to seven:
Morning again in this holiday heaven.
I quickly rose from the goose-feathered bed
Shaking sleep from both limbs and head,
Heard the cool-coo of the Summer-time dove
Answer the call of his lime-tree-love,
And dressing as fast as I possibly could
Ran down the stairs to the hall and stood
To watch the gold swing in the grandfather clock
Then hurry to breakfast and country talk.

Still if I listen I hear the sound
In the midst of the mad world whirling round,
The pendulum swing – not fast – not slow
That measured my childhood long ago.

Lambing

It all depends on the season
whether we call the high fields,
tucked in a fold in the hills,
'the garrets', because they are nearer heaven,
or the 'labour rooms' because the sheep go there to give birth.

Summer, autumn, winter, 'the garrets' suffice
but in spring the fields freshen,
spare-frost-winds whisking out dust for renewal of life
and the 'labour rooms' are ready.

On April evenings I watch sheep heavy with lamb
graze at the base of the hill
and if one wanders away from the herd to climb upward –
if one wanders away from the deep-fleeced others
there will be birth by morning
and I am there at dawn with my crook,
lambing bag, sweet annointing oil
at the attic roof of the world
with the winter-brown grass still apparent
but where green cleaves the earth.

Sometimes the sheep is delivered –
the spindle-legged lamb bonded and skipping
in air bubbling with curlews.
Sometimes there is trouble –
a shepherd's hands essential
and a heavenly worth in the journey.
Sometimes there is death –

A white rag on the frost-tipped grass
and a frantic mother.

You can't tell which you will find
before being there on the April-bare hillside
under a lark-ascending, lapwing-tumbling sky.

Farmyard Geese

They sit like rocks
Impervious to weather
And let the gale clash
Round them in the yard;
Rain, hard as silver pellets,
Hitting deep feather layers
That hardly ruffle.
Bright leaves, October crisp,
Dance round like Dervishes
Fearful and half flying –
To fall – to fly again.

Occasionally they quirk their stylish necks,
Look round but never make the slightest move
To goose step to barn-shelter,
Rather they calmly ride the storm
As flat-based-boats do –
                    – moored and barely rocking.

A Moonlight Walk in November

The owl on woollen wing
Smoothes from the dark Dutch barn
Wafting outwards
The warm rich smell of hay.
Caught in the luminous light,
A plastic cover ripples and flows
In silver waves across the straw stack,
And from the approaching pylon
A constant crackling
Vibrates the ears.

Away from unnatural noises
Thin ice scrunches a puddle,
Startles the hidden hare
Who leaps, a ghostly shadow,
On long soft foot
Across the frosted furrows.
The lonely lapwing's cry
Rouses the resting night
While grey grasses at the road verge
Whisper brittle secrets.

Midnight chimes clear
From the invisible village:
Everywhere moonlight
And wild goose music.

Strawberry Field

They cover the dark green field
In many-coloured patches,
The pickers,˙
Kneeling on earth, straw, leaves,
held in an envelope of air
Smelling of fresh-crush strawberries.

Away from the supermarket, road-rush,
Quick-green-man, they pick with ink-blue fingers
Into yellow buckets
Sometimes thrusting the pitted half-juice fruit
Through parched lips.
At lunch time they find coolness
In the shadow of a tree,
Open sticky flasks,
Eat 'pieces' made with early morning haste.

They laugh, talk, work,
It's hot, sun-splitting afternoon – they tire,
A mother clouts her daughter,
'Get off your lazy arse
Get doon that dreel and pick!'
Two bored, baked laddies flare,
Fling berry bombs
And sudden war breaks out.

A bell – a slow voice shouting 'berry-up!'
Pickers drift to the weighing-in,
Arms long to earthy leaves;

They argue, banter,
hot money falls into stained and sticky hands;
Red buses rev and wait.

In the sun
A low swallow swerves,
Catches what nourishment it can.

Oil Seed Rape

The violence of the colour
Rapes the earth,
Rape-seed field
Ripening into flower:
Like fallen sun
it dazzles the dragging clouds
That send down rain in slants
To cool the ardour.

The field lies
Abandoned yellow splash,
Subdues into submission
Living green of wheat.

Even the blue/white yachts,
Calm on the river,
Can't tempt my eye
From such fertility.

Night Work

One a.m. – the whirr of harvesters
Soothe the August night
And dragons' eyes
Light up the swathes of gold
That fall to the reapers' knives.

The night is dry, wind light,
Lone men sit in high towers,
Work before dew-fall –
Oblivious to the moon
In her opalescent shell
Shining through open windows
On to harvest widows
Hugged in silver downies.

And on children asleep
Each in a silk cocoon
Curled like pink prawns
Among the shifting shadows.

Farmers work on
Concentrate on harvest.

Go For Another Gold

The stiff land –
Difficult land, sea clay,
Home of hare and heron
Laid down aeons ago:
Drained by the monks
Coming over the hills
From the abbey
And now, year after year
With the knowledge
And hard work of man,
Grows wheat better
Than most other land.

Councillors in Cabals
    Who do not understand the land,
Wheeler dealers
  Who care nothing for the land,
The new purchasers
  Who do not love the land
Attempt to change its use
Quickly without you noticing!
And if you should protest
Pretend they do not hear.
'Go for another gold not grain:'
Not the world's future
But immediate gain:
Industrial estates,
Concrete to cover all,
Kill the land dead.

But what of tomorrow
One day, one week, one year
Too little food.

Must we be starving
To have it understood
The basic building blocks
Of life are grass and grain?

September Fires

Late evening and a light wind
Send farmers burning straw in harvest fields.
From where I stand, warm in an anorak,
I see dancing coronas, flickering gold,
Releasing smoke, the colour of sunset,
To drift and rise into
An egg shell sky.

There, beneath the hills,
A castle flares in light – is gone!
Towards the east, the three-pronged dovecot,
Centuries old, stands out in black relief.
Fires expand space, an optical illusion
But viewed from higher ground
It must look as though
The cities of the plains are burning.

Beside me, the apple orchard
holds in her dark green breath –
Daring the long sierras of fire
To come much closer;
The top of the oak tree glows with light
And farmhouse chimneys blush and pale again.

Tonight, fantastic movement, flame-red energy,
Tomorrow, stillness and the black scorched earth
cleaned and ready to take new seed
In whose dark cells . . .

Lie the germ
Of their own destruction.

Country Children

First – the fireworks –
Rockets whizzing darkwards –
A thrilling whee, a big bang,
cascades of coloured stars
parachuting down
to melt into oblivion.
Children, in the farm cart,
there for safety,
scream with pleasure and excitement.

Then it is the bonfire –
Children jump to the puddled earth
watch a woof of flame
consume a falling guy.
Afterwards food from the farm kitchen –
Sausages to frazzle, cheddar potatoes
hot in small and eager hands –
The damp November night
is palpable with energy.

Sparklers handed round
fizz in silver spires.
Wild wind reduces branches
to hills of red hot embers.
Mallows that top thin sticks,
charred and sticky.
melt in fresh mouths.
The empty twigs remaining,
pointed with fire,
become fireflies in the night
in the unseen hands of children.

In the distance, far from the children,
across the trembling blackness,
a city of amber lights
that one day may consume them.

Midnight Train

Train on the midnight track, lit by the pale moon glow
Where in the morning light, where will you be?
Bay window open wide
listening ears inside
Where are you hurrying to, where do you go?

Rumbling and rushing on, coming from Aberdeen,
Barrier crossing one field-length away
Green lights now flash for you
Train that goes dashing through
Following the moon-silver path of the Tay.

What are you carrying, oil, fish or business men?
Where do you take them, where do you stop
Is it all change at Crewe?
London perhaps for you
After these brooding hills, this dreaming glen?

New Homes

These crumbling northern nesting-barns must go
Where swallows have for centuries been drawn
from tigered veldt and Drakensbergs they know
On flight paths gened from generations gone
To where the blackthorn whitens into flower
And grass is April-green with sun and shower.

I've watched these scythe-birds from firecrest dawn
Gathering mud from every rainy pool,
Wheel about the marsh, above the lawn,
Dive below lintels into sudden cool;
There on the crossbeam rafters come to rest,
under curving pantiles build a nest.

These old red roofs are now beyond repair,
These walls of stone in every shape and shade
Must meet their fate, (the JCB's loud blare)
That once with skill, the caring craftsman made;
yet modern days and modern ways must be,
New things grow, although it saddens me.

But see – across the fields, the phoenix rise
From rubble on our nearest neighbour's place
Silver-white it leans against the skies,
Down-winged and high it has an airy grace;
Here tall-cabbed tractors are now housed at night
And swallows build fresh nests at greater height.

For nothing lives if it becomes time-trapped
And everything must die that won't adapt.

The Blackcock

We had passed through the lost valley
Yellow-gold with Autumn,
Coming eventually to the dark hill:
Here the rough witch-broom heather
Had faded, not into insipid paleness
But to something that gave
An over-all feel of black-purple.
He was waiting for us
Standing on a rotten fencepost
In an ebony elegance,
Shining silk-feathered in the sun.
He seemed as curious about us
As we about him.
Only movement the turning of his head
To show us the metallic blue of his face.
Proud fellow, he sensed our admiration.
Behind him, in the camouflage-scrub,
His wives lurked in purdah;
They too were curious about the strangers –
One shy head after another bobbing up
to have a look;
It was obvious that they
Were in awe of him
As much as we were.

Villanelle to a Bat

Under cover of the dusk the Pipestrelle
    Drifts from cobwebbed corners of the byre
To flit about the puzzled moon's strange dell.

Does he detect me? How can I quite tell?
    I see him feel the air, now low, now higher
Undercover of the dusk the Pipestrelle.

Last night I watched him as blue darkness fell
    Where insects filled the night above the myre,
Flit about the puzzled moon's strange dell.

Once I heard his piercing pitch so well
    In reedy chorus of an airbourne choir
Undercover of the dark the Pipestrelle.

Older now but still I feel the spell
    Of web-winged mouse beneath the star's pale fire
As undercover of the dusk the Pipestrelle
    Flits about the puzzled moon's strange dell.

Manx Shearwater: Rhum

In the hour before midnight
On nights that have no moon –
Extraordinary sound, from underground
On the remotest of mountains – Trollaval

Vikings came here once
When myths were more
Than fairy tales for children.
They saw through northern eyes
Trolls and goblins,
Huge or squat like Martians,
Heard the screams and cries
In the hour before midnight –
Underground.

But we who are 20th century wise,
We who are informed
Know that Trolls emerge from burrows
High on the mountain side
Transformed to dark-eyed,
Dark winged birds
Who leave single celled homes
Cradling one lone chick
To glide above grey waves
That leap like Dolphins,
To shear the water. . .

Scythe it with curved wings.

Pine Martin in Captivity

It's useless trying to get out this way –
Running round the perimeter of your cage
With low soft growlings,
Banging into all the corners,
Flinging yourself high and hard
At the netting. It must hurt.
Your companion, the longer captive,
Watching your crazy movements, knows better
But you pay her no heed, eyes closed, ears shut
As they are with jail fever.

Forgive us, your captors,
Our commitment to conserve
But you are beautiful,
Dark diamond eyes in a triangle head,
Deep browns against meadow-sweet creaming of breast.

I'm glad I've seen you today
Yet I'd rather have been surprised
By a quick glimpse of grace
From a bright rain of birch leaves
Or fast dancing limbs in the primeval pines
Whose branches even on a dull day,
Seem reddened by sunset . . .

Today, I grieve for your plight
Knowing how it feels.
I, too, battered myself against fences
Before learning that the spirit is free.

Lark Singing in a Storm

Hard to sing a love song in a storm
When snow-cold gales blow over white Craigowl,
Last week was pleasant sundrift, bright and warm
But now the sting sleet-rain pelts on the soul
Yet far above me in the lift and throbbing high
A lark sings from a waste of murky sky.

His nest drowned out, his eggs all washed and cold
He knows the pattern, he will start again
And uncomplaining will remake the mould
Oblivious to anguished loss or pain,
Though mate still shivering on the splashy ground
His hopeful song is yet a happy sound.

These water-fields will have to be re-sown
The grain that is un-chitted now will rot
An instant loch – as small waves rise, I groan
Yet sing within at austere beauty caught
And here I face the paradox again
The tug between deep happiness and pain.

Perhaps then, it is not all unique
That when disaster strikes still bliss can rise
The weather in the heart and head is freak
Nests drown, crops rot, too-early-blossom dies
But if the copious heart is filled with spring
In spite of hardship some can always sing.

Powerless

Too brief a Summer –
must it end already?
I walk where I can see
The swallows skim the barley,
And fly with them, dance with them,
Rise and fall, swoop and swerve,
Whirl in their lively fly-catch ballet,
Feel the excitement of their coming journey,
The antique call to Africa –
Until up, up, up they soar
Off into the sunset . . .

I pass acre upon acre of white-gold heads
That feather-soft and bowing gracefully
Await the harvester's inevitable whirr,
While at the fence's side
Pale grey-spun thistledown
holds very still like candyfloss,
For soon the drifting wind will come
To catch and carry it away.

Barely September
Yet a Grey Goose vanguard
Patterns the sky and autumn sound descends:
I stop awhile, happy and sad,
Humble and proud, and powerless
To halt the stalking seasons
For one split glorious second.

Pavilions

The word pavilion conjures up
Childhood growing by the sea
Summer castles all of sand,
Airy buildings roofed and free
Open to the salt and sun,
The seagull cry, slow turn of tide
And in these breezy pillared halls
There was no place for sharks to hide . . .

There are pavilions of the mind
Mysteriously of this kind.

Curious Properties

'Exhalation of flowers'
It was called,
Distilled and bottled
From brief blooms
That graced these northern moors:
Claimed it would cure anything
The body could conjure up:
And so some credulous folk believed.

It was expensive
For clear water
From a highland burn
And yet perhaps there were
strange cures –
Faith has curious properties.

No Gender

The spirit has no gender,
Is neither male nor female,
Transcending denominational
Temples such as this:
Each one of us is bound
For the same destination point,
Each one has common root
From deep dark moss of being
And the first creature crawling on the land.

First Born

After the shimmering of summer stars
and the sky's great dawning
when we sang with the speeding truck
feeling the inner storms – the promises –
thinking of prams and pushchairs
in the mild rose-garden air –

Through the red flesh you came
unlocking silences.

Random

For many years your tiny seed lay
deep in darkest earth, unmoved, unmoving,
waiting for the signal
that monitors the miracle of growth –
Seed becoming shoot
that pushes with astounding strength
through stiff clay
to where rain falls and sunshine beams for you.

First certain things must happen –
Coulter for a plough digs just that little deeper,
hoists up your amazing atom,
killer powder misses your lucky patch
        Chance –
                  Random happening –
   Your turn now!

Rise the green fuse!
Grow persistently!
Unfurl your frail and petalled hat
triumphant in poppy red!

No Promises

You didn't promise me roses,
Young and in love,
Wanting a wife, it's a wonder,
You were wise,
Wise as this solid house
That smiles and says nothing;
Expecting flowers I might have railed
Against Winters that hid them,
Run off.

This morning, in the sunlight,
The whitethroat sings in the green larch tree:
Near the edge of the clover-rich lawn
I know a stillness of roses;
At their centring heart
Snow-in-Summer
Drifts up the grey sundial
That tells time
As calmly, efficiently
As three decades ago
When you told me no lies.

Two butterflies dance
Near the Buddleia-branch
Aware of the coming blue flower,
Across the brick wall
Falls the shadow.

Villanelle for Spring

I feel an ache that was not there before
When blackbird on the blossom starts to sing
For all the lost ones I can meet no more

So many loves gone through that one-way door
That even now when gean trees glow with spring
I feel an ache that was not there before

And though dawn casts her light on earth's greenfloor
sad are the thoughts the tear-bright dew-drops bring
For all the lost ones I can meet no more

Yes, though I've found a new love I adore
Who makes the bells within me gently ring
I feel an ache that was not there before

Now earth begins again, lets loose her store
From seed and twisty wood while wild thoughts wing
For all the lost ones I can meet no more
I feel an ache that was not there before.

Loss

There is this vast silence –
Nothing more . . .

You should be here
In the kitchen – now!
With the offspring gone to bed,
Sitting in the high Windsor
That is so much a part of you.
You should be here
On this fire-out summer evening,
Drinking a last draught from banded mug,
Discussing this and that,
Wondering if the peas are ready to combine,
Asking if the yellow canary
In the window, the trailing fern, need water
Or how many of the
Speckled courgettes, glossy from the garden,
I mean to freeze for winter;
Inconsequential things
That made our days . . .

But there is this vast
Uncontrollable silence . . .
Nothing more.

Starfall

Easter – an oyster moon –
Now winter has let go her icy grip at last;

I follow my ghost-thrown shadow
Round the old farm road
Covered by kindness from the softer stars;
From the mysterious hills I hear
Sheep calling lambs with anxious tenderness;
Closer, the dark earth, worked by the frost
Waits for the scattering seed:
This late spring there is no time for sleep,
The night vibrates with bird-love,
A thrill of curlews release a throbbing cry –
I peer into the opalescent half-light
Willing myself to see outline of bird,
Moving curve of wing
But nothing is revealed except sound, sensation,
A void charged with life
And new beginnings,
Hope,
A star falls –
One lone thought of galactic grandeur drops –

What a night to die upon a cross!

Unusual Powers

A dandelion can break through tarmac,
Display its glorious suns.
A bee can bumble backwards
From warm pollen
In wallflower cups
and on frail wings
Raise its bulky body to the wind,
(Engineers will tell you this can't happen
Aerodynamics being as they are).
A small boy with a simple sling
Can kill Goliath!
A poet, a child, a minister
with some slight word
Can suddenly point through the hopeless heart
To find the hidden truth . . .

So who can say who rolled the stone away?

Preference

Sheep on the hills of April
climb singly, when their time has come,
away from the multitude
Find some windfree hollow –
give birth –
The bleating lamb part of the bearing earth;
or so it was when I was shepherding
on Sidlaw slopes

Had I been Mary,
I would rather the dim stable
to the blazing Inn
The rustling donkey to the raucous din
        and gaze of men
                But then
                        We are not told
                The preference of Mary.

Sanctuaries

The peninsula of Morven
where colour, shape astounds –
Wet lichens on the rocky splash-shore,
seapinks sheltering in crevices,
the golden samphire
flowering where it can. . .

and cradled in the rocks
still, calm pools of light,
small universes bright
with seaweeds under crystal –
frond forests, red, green, brown
where nothing moves.

But watch awhile –
That small pyramid
you could not prise from rock – walks:
Winkles in small houses slide along:
Remove a frond of kelp
and gently prod
one of these ruby globes
and watch how sea anemone,
waiting for the tide,
unfolds its velvet arms. . .

True sanctuaries are within
deep rock pools in the mind
to touch in time of trouble –
If you can journey there
home can be anywhere.

The Inner Citadel

Eventually all of us
Should adventure
Down into ourselves:
When the living and loving
Has quietened
We should take the journey
Into the dark interior,
Down, down, down
Past Aladdin's cave
And the vivid stars
To find at the core
The inner citadel;
It is always there,
In everyone . . .
Waiting.

He Came With three Things

He came with his dog,
His clock,
His picture of Durisdeer –
And made our lives richer.

His collie runs with swift grace,
Rounds up dream sheep,
Drops stones at our feet;
Head lowered and forward
Can keep perfectly still
Poised on tight springs
Ready to run in any direction.

His clock, a grandfather,
Melts dark polished colour
Into the corner.
Has it always been there?
Slow gold gleam
On its old brass face
Gives certain light;
The tick and the tock
Are unhurried and sure;
Chimes at the hour
Certain and mellow.
Graven lettering reads
Isaac – Elizabeth Lancafter,
Porthoufe, Penrith –
How long ago were the 'Ss' all 'Fs'?

And the picture?
Each morning I wake,
See on the wall
Wild poppies blowing,
Watch passing deep clouds
Above soft-coloured hills
Protecting a village –
Days begin calmly.

Nasturtiums

Common flowers I called them,
Hardly noticing how they grew.
Other, fancier blooms
Eclipsed their glory . . .

Until this Spring –
Seeing them grow against the white wall
At the gable end of the farm house
With no other flowers in sight,
I think how lovely they look –
How bright, rich, warm
In orange, yellow, red
Trailing stems along the ground
In bridal bouquets,
Climbing harled stone,
Sheltering silk trumpets under leaves
Like miniature green umbrellas
Holding silver balls of rain.

Perhaps I notice them more
Because you planted them,
Care about them.
I remember your pleasure
When the first tiny plant
Pushed through the soil.
(You took me from the warm kitchen
Into the wind and rain
To see the miracle.)
And always, when passing,
You look to see
What progress they have made,
How tall they are becoming.

The day you picked me the first flower
I put it in a clear glass bowl
And noticed that, like you,

It had a happy morning face –
Not trying to be grand or anything,
Not seeking admiration.

Autumn in Glenprosen

Here buzzard and blackcock
With grey feathered feet,
Here mountain and river
And landscape all meet,
Beyond the arched rainbow
On this narrow way
October's bright shoes
Have crept lightly today;
Soft colours imposed
On a sepia print
Of bleak barren winter no skeletal hint,
Beeches and birches
In sun-enthralled gold
Find russets of bracken
Its greenness grown old
And lonely grey houses
Half hidden by hill
With smoke signals leaping
All other things still . . .

Past Summer's high rainbow
I cannot yet see
But I hope that, as gently,
The Autumn finds me.

Back to Basics

Man . . .
The idea,
The beginning,
The green force that drives,
Turner of the wheel,
Protecting shield,
Tender of sheep on the storm mountain,
Catcher of fish under high wave,
Digger of peat on the windy moor,
Hunter in the dark wood,
The bearer of good gifts
Back to the black house . . .
His mandala.

Woman . . .
Hub of the wheel,
Mistress of the wide skirt
That little children cling to,
The warm peat fire at the black house core,
Girdle that bakes oatmeal cakes,
Iron pot on the sway,
Spurtle that stirs . . .

She is . . .
Sun gold flower
That becomes the white clock . . .
Punctured cushion that's left
When parachutes fly.

Water – Wood – Stone

Go to make a meal mill –
Stone from the mountain,
Wood from the forest,
Water from the river
A constant inch of it
To turn the wooden wheel.

Grain from the Glen –
And I remember
Oatmeal in the girnel,
Brose for breakfast,
Oatcakes on the girdle
Over the peat-fire flame.

We watch the great wheel turn,
Hear water rush away.
See the kiln that dries
The oat to nutty flavour,
Tall bins that hold,
Small buckets that lift to attic floor,
Sieves removing straw,
Cockle drum catching weedseeds.

Oats drop,
Dust drifts through dust-harp,
Groats go to grinding stones,
The meal they make to mouths. . .

Blood, muscle, bone.

Holiday Cottage

On its own the old farm cottage stands
    facing the peaceful fields where cattle graze.
The morning Buzzard scours its chosen lands,
    his home the air above green swards that raise
to close horizons, banks of blazing broom,
    rocky outcrops, hawthorn in heady bloom.

It's snug and trig inside. The panelled pine
    gives off a satin glow. A wall of brick
and stone surrounds the warm black stove. We dine
    off willow pattern. Cottage walls are thick
keep out the Solway wind. We like the rain
    that runnels gently down the window pane.

Today the rain recedes. The morning haze
    lifts from field and hill and at the door
the Yellow Hammer spends familiar phrase.
    A day to dance in sunlight – to explore
forest and firth while healing nature strives
    to furbish up worn fabric of our lives.

Strangers in Skye

Stuck as the limpets to their rocky pools
So are the houses on this peaty moor,
Clear as sea water changed with each sure tide
So is the air around this turning sphere,
Blue as the sea, White as the flying spray
So is the sky above our eager heads.

Still is the waiting underwater life,
Only the aqua-heather almost flows,
Still is the patient purple-hearted earth
Only we move watched by the hidden eyes,
All else seems held in crystal quietness,
This living world, pulses down-drawn
Waits for the stranger on this Isle to pass.

Northern Midsummer

It's never really dark
here in the Hebrides
In June;
The bird has hardly lost its tune
When it sings again.

Two a.m.
Daylight fades
But see – a strange glow
Hovers hawk-winged
Waiting behind those hills,
Watching the silver throw of moonlight
Move over seal-rocked sea loch,
heron-homed islets.

Three a.m.
A blackbird, re-entering the fray,
Gathering dawn together,
Carols day.

A Strange Flower at Loch Sunart

Relic from the ice age,
Delicate lichen-flower
Modestly rising on a hirsute stem
from frilly grey-blue bed
Topping the rotting deer-post

Dripping December,
The sun flirts out
To flash on grey rock,
Light each tiny rainball
Hanging from slim wands
Of red/mauve birch trees:
Underfoot, a rich red/russet
Tangle of wet dead fronds,
Summer's trumpeting bracken:
Here and there,
Cushions of emerald sphagnum.

No other flower about, only you!
Palest cream and dish-shaped,
Edged with finest hairs
Like rays from a white dwarf –
Saying I am that I am,
Proclaiming this air free from impurities.
I think of similar shape –
Dishes that reflect from Telstar.

Seeing you, small pre-historic flower,
Thrills me more
Than had I been in Madagascar
When fishermen found the coelacanch.

Mingary

The road now led through wilderness
    We'd left the brilliant trees behind;
Across the rain soaked moors we drove,
    Watching the switchback trail unwind
Before us like some pale-backed snake,
    Down to where earth and sea combined.

The moors were yellow-russet gold
    The sky a slate-stone-quarry grey
That did not manage quite to take
    The feel of sun and warmth away
Until we reached the great grey sea
    And the rock bound shore at Mingary.

Where fabled castle dark and still
    Stood watching from the lonely bay
As shadowy Islands came and went
    In the fickle light of drowning day;
Where waves rolled slowly and slowly in
    And time lost meaning at Mingary.

Experimental Seafish Station, Ardtoe

Each a scalloped universe –
They lie motionless in trays –
Wild spat collected in western Kyles
And brought to holding tanks.
We contemplate the stillness
And then one stone-like shell,
A secret Queen inside,
Comes skimming to the surface
And swims, mysteriously to eyes,
That do not see the inner jet propulsion.

The separated Kings keep to the tank's dark bottom,
Are returned to watery habitat where they hang
In pearl then in lantern nets,
Grow to market size –
Man trying to farm the ocean
Against nature's awesome forces.

Lobsters as tiny as tadpoles
With ventral fins and swishing tails,
Swim in glass bowls.

In a green lean-to
Long plastic bags of watered algae
Bubble with tubed air
And on the shelf opposite, microscopes
Show tiny forms of life, krill
Complete with square egg packets
Perfect in design.

Under an attic roof we walk a plank – look down
On halibut in huge round pool –
Squashed worlds in every shade of grey
That glide with upward-looking eyes;
Stock, bred or captured from the stormy seas
To milk of precious eggs.

Open day but the hatchery is closed
To prying eyes
Where thousands will burst to life
At ten past three . . .

Outside a great grey world
Of rock and sea
Obeys the oldest rhythms.

Calgary Bay

It was probably raining
When they left Mull
And there must have been weeping.
Standing on the beach,
Semi-circling the bay in palest gold,
I can feel tears in the wet wind.
Some left to make a new Calgary
Thousands of miles across an ocean,
Deep in the heart of land waves,
Frozen in winter.
They could see in the distance
Mountains higher and rockier
But not these green baize hills,
And their homes were not
These lonely cottages
With solemn eyes on the sea.

It's quiet here now.
My mind drifts backwards
A century or more
To those people making way for sheep.
I watch the emigrants leave:
In little boats they make for the big ship
With white sails.
Some get caught in the rip tide
Which almost pulls them back.
The anchor lifts,
There's weeping on shore and ship.

Today there's only the staccato bleating
On the hillside,
The lonely children of early tourists
Running on salty feet,
Wrestling with the wind,
Making castles they hope won't break
In a welter of sea. . .

And where the crescent thins to nothingness
A sandpiper calls from the black boulders.

Walk with all Seasons

I need to walk with the Winter as well,
Need to stride in the wind's authority
That booms under the pylon, jets along power lines,
Drives down the creek in rough crinkles,
Roars through the leafless tree,
Wheels through my hair, twisting it over my face,
Frosting my ears, shoving me hard along.

Veering – I bend into the gale,
A cloud-curtain rips, the sun rushes out
To shine along new satin furrows:
On the last of the stubble a thousand geese feed,
Rise when I get too close;
Each bird, for a moment,
Gives in to the tug-of-war wind
Swings back low overhead
In strong glory of light and dark grey,
Sun caught and cloud captured at once.

I stroll with the conjuring Spring,
Somersault Summer, curfew of fall
But I must have weight of the wind, the struggle,
Walk with the Winter as well
Before I am whole.

Fishing for Pearls

Kenneth C Steven

*For Uncle Donald, for whom Blair Atholl, Perthshire
and all of rural Scotland mean so much*

Sabbath

That day the air was different. The fields lay under the sky
Not breathing; the sun above them
Broke like a glass vase, spilled bits of light
Over the long dark edge of the moor.

The farms lay in their own lands
As if somehow in a vast cathedral, still
In the presence of their Creator.

No tractors rambled out across the Easter acres;
No teenage cars, thudding with rock and roll
Slammed along back roads.
Only a few peewits rose and swivelled,
Their high song carrying eerily
In a wind, an endless wind.

Through the window I saw them going to church –
All in black, their suits and hats
Immaculate. The rain slanted
From a bruise of cloud; the women scuttled
Fastening flapping hats to their heads
With Bibled hands.

I went outside
Into the worshipping of the larks
The thanksgiving of the spring.

The Cathedral

When lights lemon the river in June
And the river is so low a boy could plash across,
Barbecues glow along the banks, their meat
Dribbling and crackling. If you go upstream –
The dusk sky blue, the clearest liquid blue –
If you go barefoot as far as the cathedral,
You will see the bats tipping and flitting the water
Like pieces of muslin, the air rank with their scent.
Their wings click as they turn, as they nip midges
Softly weaving patterns through the trees
Till milky, stars come out, and it is dark at last.

Remember

It is also about the small things:

Being woken by sunlight,
The cherry scent of the springtime.

Going into the morning forest to cut logs,
The sun slanting like beams from the sky.

Feeding a robin in February snow,
Listening to the bright jewellery of his song.

Watching a child coming home from school
With an armful of chestnuts and a long story.

Listening to the great spirit of the wind
Wrestling with the trees all through the night.

Laughing at the huge thrashing of rain,
Running and laughing through the autumn rain.

Otter

He is a traveller with no fixed abode –
The most restless beast in all the world,
A lover in every port.

Never built for land, a bumping thing,
Uncomfortable and overdressed,
Desperate to flow back to water.

Listening to the wind, he knows
The tick of a salmon's tail upstream
From the thud of a man.

In his element, let loose,
A Celtic brooch of knots and coils,
A circle without end.

Roads have driven him away;
He moonlights through silent rivers
No louder than the felt wings of bats.

When we have gone, after fire or flood,
And the world returns to before, he will come back,
A rune in every river.

The Day the Earth was Flat

I go there still, in my mind
Down half a dozen autumns to the place
We picked potatoes. Through a lens of rain
The fields slide flat, boots suck
Up to the shins in mud. The travellers watch,
Skinned the colour of ripe horse chestnuts,
Eyes like unbroken horses', their language
Hot as whisky. They'd rather spit at us than talk.
The tractor rambles on across the field
Its bad lungs smoking, then suddenly,
Around our feet are shells, soft lumps that drum
Into the buckets. All our backs are hunched
Along the line of hours that drizzle on
Till farm lights start to home the dusk
Across the valley. We walk back crippled,
Slumped sacks too tired for talk. Only Jo
Sparks up the firefly of a cigarette
And lets us suck its dizzy sweetness;
Dave brings a golden bottle from his bag –
We drink pure pain and nodding, call it bliss.
I see us still back there, all walking onwards into men
Our world no wider than that one potato field
Our world as flat, our fears no bigger.

The Forest

Once upon a time the trees
Breathed green this land.

There was no gap, no gash
In a garment that reached the sea.

All the songs were wood, all the wolves
Were songs, and no paths, no roads

Cut. Through that glade the light glowed
The rain grew. An emerald,

A huge jewel, ringing with many greens,
A jade scent, a lemon air, a noise of serpentines,

Day and night. Until the time we stumbled on this earth,
Slashing as we went, burning our way

Into an empty future, a cleared waste.

Night Without Darkness

It is June in the Hebrides –
The skies are blue and green, luminous,
Late at night, and I wait awake
By an open window watching.

I cannot stop listening to the silence;
I hear it at midnight and cannot sleep.
I lie and wonder, and this giant quiet,
Big as the Atlantic, fills the room.

The sea rises like soft glass,
The moon climbs in a ball of cobwebs,
The stars light like river pearls –
The night and the morning are one.

Wasps

That August the wasps invaded
Like a gang of bikers.
In their yellow and black jackets
They drizzled the air, zoomed around corners.

In the endless hot blue afternoons
They crawled into jam and across plates,
Bashed windows and went at full throttle
Around cafes and swarms of tourists.

Until one day the skies turned orange
And the air hung in misty curtains,
Heavy and hot as wool. Very far away
Thunder prowled about the hills like bears.

A gull sailed away making a sound
Like an old bicycle wheel; a bit of lightning
Squirmed above the woods, and suddenly,
Rain began falling in great grapes.

Next morning, the wasps were dead;
Outside hotels and shops their crisp hulls lay
Like curled leaves. They blew away
Through the lanes, were washed into wet September ditches.

Midnight Sun

The boat furled out in a pale hum
Over water clear as glass
A whole half hour. Then the engine melted.

Nothing. Just the mountains inland
Torched by sunlight, just five gulls
Dipping near us, leaving pearls.

We pulled twenty fish from the heavy timelessness of that water,
Dragged them flapping, gaping for air,
Into the huge blue light of July.

Over them the water shut once more
Like the biggest door in the world. We turned at last,
Ploughed home through blood and salt.

Meeting

Today I met a journeyman thatcher.
He had not been born with that life in his blood;
One day he just dug up his roots and left,
Never looked back.

He said that sometimes as he swept the thatch
Up onto a roof and heard the shingle of the trees,
The fields' chase, he was blown
Out of the mad motorway of this age

To a place that you never could buy,
A place that is on no map.
He had heard it and touched it in roofs,
In thatch, just once or twice, for a moment.

In him now the back lanes, the side roads
Of a timeless time, a land where hay ricks
Still jolt and topple. I sensed the sunlight in him
Warm as a whole summer.

The Wood

The wood is a well. Like lips
The trees close tight. This is summer –
June, the keystone of the year.
In here, inside the wood, the flies are strumming,
They crawl over a cut pine like molten lava.
Sunlight washes the forest floor,
A kind of honey, spins and circles
In eternal dancing. A twig bangs broken,
Six mauve-soft doves flutter upwards,
Melt into the sky. The trinkets of a stream
Wink and chatter far away.
The shadows of the wood are cool,
They smell of mushrooms, of ancient leaves,
Of dead owls.

Breakfast

A trout caught from a Highland river,
A half foot of struggling;
Thumped on the head, the eye clouds.
A knife slips through the fish, making two flaps;
Inside, the flesh is pink,
Like a sunrise.

Hissed into the pan over an orange fire
On an emptiness of moorland in June,
It comes out all crisp and brittle,
Stinging with salt and lemon.
Miles above, a buzzard swims
Like a log in a blue pool.

Wild Goose Chase

Under a bridge
Something like a print.

A paw, perhaps, passed by
At midnight, padding

North, and leaving
Just a hint of fish.

Trail all day
Catch glances, ripples

That could be
Might be

A piece of an otter
Playing Houdini

Melted into water
Gone to ground.

Skye

Burns Talisker from the hills
And pools run dark as pure cairngorm.
The bracken is turning the colour of foxes,
The air burns with the scent of peat.

The Atlantic combs the coast, white and wild,
Seabirds steer the high wind.
Up on the ramparts of the Cuillin
An eagle is flying at half-mast.

The Mushrooms

We drove all the way to Foss
On a blue, blustery morning for mushrooms;
Past the church to the edge of the loch
Till there in the last field –
White hats, whole villages of them, far into the trees.

We beat silver paths through the grass to get there;
Broke whole slabs of mushrooms in our hands
That were pink underneath, delicate with petticoats,
Smelling of loam, of the very heart of autumn,
Walked back to the car laden with great white moons.

Later with butter they scuttered and sang in the pan
And we ate them reverently, thankfully, blessing their coming
Another autumn, another year.

The Slide

We longed for the sharp crinkle of December stars,
That ghostly mist like cobwebs in the grass –
Ten degrees below zero.

After the snow came petalling from the skies,
Settled into a deep quilt, the frost
Diamonded the top, making a thick crust.

On the long descent of the lawn
We made our slide, planed the ground
Hour after hour till it smiled with ice.

At night we teetered out with buckets,
Rushed the water down the slide's length
In one black stain.

Next day the slide was lethal,
A curling glacier that shot us downhill
In a single hiss.

Even after the thaw greened our world again
The slide remained written in the grass
As long as our stories.

The Last Wolf

The last wolf in Scotland is not dead
Only sleeping.

He is no shaggy dog story
In the corries and crags of Cairngorm.

He is never in danger of being killed,
But rather dying of neglect.

If the last wolf promised to renounce violence
He would be allowed to lie by any peat fire in Scotland.

But his paws keep the memories of battles
And there is smoke in the grey of his eyes.

He has waited here two hundred years and more
For a blizzard that might flay the summer

From our soft hands and old excuses.

In my Father's Time

He saw the airships glow over Glasgow
The first planes whine with asthma.
He saw the hungry years before Hitler
Rose his hand over Europe's peace.
He saw action in Germany, crossed the Rhine
Came back to the sackcloth and ashes of Auschwitz.
He heard the crack of the atom
The bomb that came soft as a kiss on Hiroshima.
He saw a man on the moon
And the globe roll round to war, big as the bang
That built the beautiful world.
Now he stands at the window watching
Wondering if he and the end will meet.

My People

In the middle of London, suddenly,
I think of them. In Garve and Achnasheen
I have seen their footprints as I passed –
I have touched their shadows.

My grandmother, my great uncles, all those of my mother's people
I never knew. They are more real to me
Than the loud rush hours of people
That hurry and jostle these streets.

All that remain of them
Are black and white photographs, faces
That slowly lose their names, their blood;
Yet they are alive, their spirits breathe.

In the middle of London
I scent the myrtle, I hear the risings of curlews,
I am back with them in the land that imprints my hands
That is written across my soul.

I keep the few stories of them I was given
Like jewellery, priceless, things of gold and silver
In a locked box. I will give its key
To my children, I will show them where it is hidden.

The Umbrella Days

How we used to quarrel in the rain –
You crying in among red traffic, all alone
Our promises broken
A hub of engines and the smell of faded tempers.

I'd run to catch you up and shine
The rainbow of a smile from your November eyes
And then we'd kiss perhaps, a smudge of make-believe
Left stranded on my cheek. I miss you now
Wherever all the mad umbrella days have gone.

The Sea

That day after the rain turned the river to a dash of gravel
We drove down to the sea,
Past the villages that lay like clamshells in the sunlight,
By little single track roads of sand
That wound down to the wide blue basin of the sea.

That day the sea smelled of the fields,
Of hay and loam, of inland and the rain,
Not salty but sweet,
And I believed as I smelled it
It would taste fresh and good if I drank it.

Peggy

The house lay on the hillside
Among daffodils and buttercups. The high snow
Had gone; the river blundered down the hill
White and breathless, so cold it hurt the hand.

The key slept where it always had, under the second slate,
Rusty, the colour of bracken.
Inside, the house smelled strange after winter –
Of sleep and dust and silence.

The crisp carcases of flies on their backs
Filled the windowpanes, last summer
Flown from their wings and forgotten.

I lit a fire in the grate but the flames
Were old and slow, like ghosts,
The wind searched through the chimney without finding.

Everywhere I went Peggy was not there;
The absence of her death hurt,
Breathed in the beating of the rowans,
Whispered among the grass stems bent and bowed
Under the wind's chasing.

And yet
She was more alive than ever before,
She was everywhere, she had become the place she loved.

The Last Day of May

All day it rained, the river drifting east like mist,
The town huddled into shrouds.
At eight suddenly before it darkened,
A breach came in the cloud, a deep rift,
Long as a continent, and behind, the swimming of blue.

We went out cautiously, walked to the water,
And by now the whole sky was clearing
As if with panes of stained glass to make a ceiling,
And the moon stood out white
As the pale round of a barn owl's face.

In that light, moths came furring over the river,
Soft things pale as pollen,
Rising in thick clouds through moonlight,
The swallows ticking and flitting among them
Like millions of scissors.

The Onion Man

In the summer
When everything was butterflies and sunlight
A Frenchman left his bicycle at an angle by the gate
Whistled down the path to the house
With ropes of onions wrapped around his neck.

My mother bought them, that year as the year before,
While I hovered in the white gold of the porch,
Watching, no taller than where his big hand
Stretched to shake my mother's own.
His words were made of white bread, of soft loam,
When he said *Bonjour* his voice filled with colours
I had never seen before:
Terracotta blue and bright ochre,
They dizzied my head with a strange journey.

I ran with him to the gate to say goodbye
Listened to the whirr of his bicycle
All down the bump of the track
Till it was lost in the summer's haze.

August Night, the Hebrides

We crabbed down through the deep seaweed
Our faces in a mesh of drizzle, so thin
It was like a smur of insects.
The water in the bay was glass, the yachts
Iced with silence. We nosed our own boat inwards
Till it thudded on the rocks,
Crouched on the swaying seats,
Hummed the engine into life
And skirled out in a single white comb,
Further and further, till the waves began to sweep
And the rain hit in splinters. I watched
A raven slouch in shrouds across a headland,
Gulls scuttering up from a white raft,
Their mouths angry. Looking back towards the land,
Lewis hunched like some ancient hump-backed whale,
Nothing but bone and rows of teeth,
Left for ever in the rattle of the Atlantic.

Sea Urchins

They are jewellery boxes from Atlantis;
Oval things – mauve and ebony and green –
Washed up already splintered by the stones
In little painted panels.

Once a fisherman brought me one from his nets
All spined like a water hedgehog.
I didn't know how to clean it
Left it three days in a bucket
Till it stank like a whole harbour.

I found my own one once. A tiny thing
No bigger than a child's clenched fist
All starred and studded, deep in a rock pool
Up out of the hammer of the sea.

It weighed no more than a wren's egg.
I carried it home through the wind's tugging
As if it were purest gold.

The Storming

All night the wind has bullied us
Thrashing the trees, booming from beneath the hills
Riding a wild rain through the morning dark.

I went out for kindling and stepped sideways
Among tightropes of storm, my face grazed
By the sudden blows. All along the hill
Woods hissing and waving, crows like ashes
Thrown away.

I swam backwards towards the door
Battled inside; deep anchors groaned and dragged
Beneath my feet.

The power lines are down across the valley;
We have returned to long before,
Our radios and televisions dumb beasts
Crouched in the candlelight.

How quickly the books come back
And the ancient words around the fire.

Capenoch Mains

The house slept down at the bottom
Of a banging of old roads.
In July it was greened by ancient oaks and beeches;
It lay in its own century, out of reach of the zoom
And batter of the towns.

Early sunlight splayed the courtyard that was knobbled with stone.
I padded there barefoot, stood
Imagining the Border horses
That once had shone there, chestnut and ebony,
That sparked these cobbles and galloped
Into ballads of brave madness.

I walked on through deep grass
Sworded with dew, further
Into the first trees, and felt a great door
Close behind me. I wanted Wallace
To ride back, to flicker through history,
Crying freedom. I saw instead
The mauve pigeons, the pale trinkets of streams,
A jewellery of sunlight on the forest floor.

Every night I took a yellow curve of lantern
Upstairs to my attic room. In the windows
Ten billion bits of crystal fired and gemmed the sky,
The huge face of an old woman rose over the hills
In the moon. I blew out the light and dared not breathe;
I listened to this world within a world,
Watching me like a guardian, like an ancient father,
And the soft, muffled ghost of an owl
Haunting my sleep with his voice.

Somewhere

The wood smells of fungus.
It does not move;

In the still sunlight
A wren makes songs out of silver

And a little bit of stream
Blinks into the loch.

Somewhere a house is burning peat
And three children are laughing,

Playing hide and seek –
Their voices like water.

Stories

I don't mean the monstrous stories
That are sold to the papers and tourists,
Which are wrapped in tartan ribbon,
And marketed from Hong Kong to California.

I mean stories that come out in crofts,
Miles across moorland after dark and whisky,
Stories that are dark as lochs and ancient;
Of creatures and sightings and strange lights – and no solutions.

Science cannot reach these crofts
To analyse and dissect such stories;
Their machinery and vehicles and equipment
Would sink into the bogland and disappear.

It takes someone to go on foot, not in a straight line,
But wandering between the tussocks to find a dry path;
A listener to hear and store the other stories,
The other history, the other science.

I went in childhood to listen;
I bottled stories in my mind and they have distilled,
When they have become pure as the peat water itself,
I will pour them for my children.

The Goose

All day there had not been a breath of wind.
The skies hung useless
The river breathed towards the sea,
Wide with autumn.
Then at dusk I heard a noise,
A single bagpipe, and high above
The smoky village and the first rose lights
I saw a goose, a single greylag
Labouring across the skies,
The stories of summer, a whole great tundra
Loud in his wings.

Dawnwatching

At ten past six my father woke me.
Ice grinned along the steps, in potholes on the track,
Stars banged in a black sky. We marched out
Across the moor towards the hillside. I missed my footing,
Crashed into bog and knives of freezing streams,
My eyes still lead with sleep. The sheepdog
Fleeced on ahead of us, flowing through the moor,
One tousled torrent. The hilltop gained we stopped,
My breath still burning in my chest.
We crouched down, faced the east, not speaking;
A curlew rose from the valley, floated out, crying,
And somewhere a car hummed up a road and disappeared.
Bit by bit the eastern hills turned grey,
The stars began to float like pearls. Beneath,
Beyond, great rents and tears grew wider in the sky,
They filled with blood, then pink, until at last,
A single thread of light still pale and faltering climbed through
And others followed, here and there, and there,
Until in one great majesty of gold
The sun broke from the dark and dawn began.

A Fishing Rod and Whisky

When the electronics of the world
Begin to wire my soul

I go upstream, twenty miles,
To a long grey raise of hills

And walk until I am tired.
A blue thread of river

Crashes there in pure waterfall;
Beyond, the moor slips away to sky.

When the dark comes I listen to the stars
I catch snatches of the water's talk.

Slowly I start to hear the trees,
Bit by bit I find I can translate the breeze.

At last, after so long out of earshot,
I begin to understand what silence means.

Gathering Sloes

After the first frost
The land is jagged;
The hills are cut like broken glass
Their tips sharp with snow.

I march along the farm track
Hands swollen huge and red
My feet squeaking on ice,
Breath dragoning the air.

I have come for the sloes –
Berries the colour of bruises –
Besieged by thorns, by sharp spears
That jab and tingle, draw little beads of blood.

In the kitchen's cool, dark hold
The sloes are gored one by one
By a skewer, then sunk in a half bottle of gin
That is left to sleep high on a scullery shelf.

Every day the bottle is turned
Till Christmas. The finished liquid is red
Full of all the ripeness of the hedgerows –
The blood of autumn.

Loch of the Lowes

The snow has left, its quartz boulders
Have turned watery at the knees and drummed seawards
Leaving the slopes washed, under frail green
And the sheep heavy with lambs.
Tufts of heather smoke are dragged into the wind
From the chimneys of the farms tucked
In the lee of woods and bits of hill.
Underneath, the loch lies like a skid of ice,
Swans nodding and dipping, mallard squabbling,
Ruffling the mirror, geese rising up in restless stretches,
Longing for Iceland. Soon the ospreys will return,
Nest in their thatch of pine – white eagles
With iron hooks in their feet –
God in their wings.

Butterfly

All winter the tortoiseshell had slept in the cupboard's dark;
Two folded halves, like a child's hands in prayer.
Now, with the new year melting,
With the daffodils buttering the field
And a great scythe of sunlight glancing across the valley
She awoke.

The blue embroidered edges of her wings
Tipped on the windowsill.
She fluttered against the glass like petals;
I put one trembling finger out – she climbed aboard,
No heavier than a dead leaf in autumn.

The sun swam through our world again
And I scraped open the window,
Held out the tortoiseshell till she lifted into April,
The start of her journey,
The one summer of her flight.

Thistles

Like Pictish warriors, thick-skinned
Armed to the teeth with daggers
They sway whispering on the hill's crown.

After losing the battle of autumn
The amethyst bonnets fray,
Their weapons start to rust.

The seed of their children
Balloons away on the wind's edge
Lighter than the feather of a wren.

Autumn Morning

Last night the first frost came.
Now the skies are blue, but not like June,
More as a lake sheened over white with ice.
Around a corner of the river the trees stand lit
In autumn fires: gold, amber, scarlet, rose,
And not the slightest hush of wind to stir them.
For a child's handful of days it will be like this,
Before the gales scatter the leaves, and wild rain
Drains the colours to the distant sea.
Bury each memory of such mornings
Deep in your soul.

Fox Cub

At the bottom of the field
That yellow-scented morning, first August,
The fox cub, coated in gold and red,
Tumbling about among bees and scents,
The bramble eyes watching.

All these years I'd waited
On the dark rim of forests, staring
For a patter of fox, an autumn patch
Out on a dawn patrol. All I heard
Were the gunshot tales of keepers,
The banged pride of the foxes
They hung from their walls.

That morning I was the one
Shot by the sudden fox –
The wry slyness of timing.

Summer

white nights of wide open windows the river thin
the curlews like pearls with their trails
the restlessness sleeping not sleeping for swallows

this longing for forests green wells like a dousing
emerald cool and delicious the swim under leaves
huge huge skies in the shingling light

the deep into water diving blue bell of the sea
drift home at dusk the swimsuit all crackled
on verandahs watch the sun fall in an orange

Awakenings

I walked in the February fields;
Crumbs of peewits rose up weeping,
Tractors rumbled about smoking like red beetles.
In the walls there were alcoves of snowdrops –
Nuns in prayer. Water came tripping and dancing
From every corner of blizzard there'd been, the songs
Our ancestors heard, the men who made circles of stone.

At the farm, collies rabbled and squealed,
Black and white bouncing, their long mouths rapping,
Tongues pink as bacon.
The yard smelled thick and yellow,
Slushed with dung – cows strutted from deep inside
Made horns of noise. A delicate shack of bones
Rubbed against me, purring, and I bent,
Listening to the rivers pouring out stories of snow.

Heading for home, I saw the fields buttered with gold
As now through the clouds the sun splayed down
And I thought –
This is the land that lay slave to winter awake.

The Dawn of the First of May

I woke creased with dreams
A shrivel of face struggling in sunlight
And my father whiskering close words of hurry.

Milkmaids had brought the dawn
Scoured the valley barns with water-clear white –
The sky was thatched with birds.

In the wood we nodded through green-heavy silence
Till a pheasant's carronade and loaded hubbub of wings
And an owl floating soft as moss to sleep.

Struggling through grass I found the river
Cleared my eyes in the water of May.

Seeing

There will be only a few days like this –
The low sun flinting the house
Through the green sea of the trees as you stand
Struck, blessed, bathed in the same light
That rose life once from the young earth, that appled
The first child's cheeks.
There will be only a few days like this
To stop doing and stand, blinking,
As the leverets tumble in the bright field,
And a cuckoo's moss voice calls from a far wood.
Wait until the sun has gone in broken orange
Down beneath the hills, and the blue sky
Hurts with the sudden shudder of the dusk.
Give thanks and turn and go back home –
For there will be only a few days like this.

The Pearl Fisher

I

In the beginning the river is a glad jug
Clanking with white water, a cold so deep
The pain stabs. All winter the gruff voice
Rushes under bridges, snows the banks.

Sometimes December has clenched a fist
So hard the water creaks with ice;
Volleys of children spill onto slides
Their mouths sending scarves of breath.

After the snow has slushed, the high churns
Come trailing over rocks in thick bunches;
The river is turned to beer, swills out wide
In drunken flows across the fields.

Come summer and the long gold days
The river has nowhere to go, but drifts into pools
Speechless, so thin the boulder ribs
Stand out all hard and starving.

Sometimes a jewel flees upstream
Fast as a skiffed stone, blue and green,
A chip of sky that turns like stone
Into a kingfisher's light.

Otters used to trundle on the banks,
Dissolve in rings of water. The cubs would tangle
Here and there in the rosy morning light,
But they have almost gone, the world too loud.

Dogs were sent to scratch them from their holts;
Noses swaying, they found the scent and leapt,
Tongues dangling like hot, wet meat,
Till the otter lost and the river bled.

Sometimes I come to watch the water,
Sudden scuffles of duck that rose upstream,
Or the shudder of a salmon ballooning up
To pink the surface for a fly.

There are fishermen on every shore,
Flicking the whips of their lines over pools
For the sudden struggling of silver –
Each year the fish are dwindling.

Maybe fox cubs the colour of bracken
Scrap and bark on these jade banks,
Ease their thirst in the first hours
Before the banged anger of the farms.

In the night the river's a snake
Hissing towards the sea. Up above
In the wild acres of the sky
Curlews compose their laments.

II

Once an osprey lord came down
From the rusty waste of the moor,
Skidded onto a long ledge of water
And carried out a salmon's flapping.

Now and then there's poaching;
Blazed headlights on a far bank,
Fish heads staring stupid in the light of day,
The cluck of gossip in every street.

Herons stand guard like grey old men
Hunched in their raincoats. Now and again
They dagger a flicker of fish
Stand fat with a lump in their throats.

Once I swam there, an early morning,
A sugaring snow on the Highland screes,
And the river knifed me, dragged out breaths
Till my head sang and the blood whirled.

I clawed out like a whittled bone
Pooled on the bank. The first sun spires
Prickled westwards from the spring dawn,
And there in the field, I saw the girls laughing.

But a knife cut me that day
Out of the shell of myself, the spun dust
Of those grey school years, it turned
To the white clear laughter of pearl.

III

I have never known where the mussels lay
The colour of slates. I have asked too often
And now the question lies on a high shelf
There with my childhood, out of reach.

Once I asked a traveller who had fished the river;
His eyes were wet with whisky, his hands lost,
But a strange shining blazed his face
Like the morning sun pooled down on water.

He did not know, or he would not tell me,
And I wondered if the fishers were all dead
Who had snagged the mussels and brought to light
The curled white shells of pearls.

Often in dream I have swayed through water
As deep as ripe wheat, my arms stabbed down
To pick the beds. But in the morning
The river's dry, the pearls all rolled to dust.

I am still searching them, the last men
Who crash through the thick, green banks
And wade out into tarry pools, or the white lash
Knowing the secret reaches.

They are black and white pictures
In the backs of books, their stories
Are pressed in the old people's heads
Like strange flowers.

I have gone back to them and demanded answers,
I have opened their stubborn eyes
And found in these memories, dormant and lost
Backwaters of pearls.

IV

The river runs the honk and jostle of Dundee,
The night sweat, the hot lights,
The furry wings of helicopters
Like moths in the dark sky.

By then the river is a poor reflection of itself,
Rainbowed with oil, a fluttering of rubbish,
Drifting out thickly to the hums of tugs,
Lightships and the rigs.

Bridges cross like iron necklaces;
In the nights their fires are jewelled
And under slide the loaded barges,
Drifting smoke far out to sea.

Here at the last wide stretches,
Aerodromes of birds are harsh with wrangling;
Torn paper gulls, long arguments of geese,
Worrying about landing in loud Icelandic.

Only little twigs of ballet dancers tiptoe here –
Plovers, curlews, high-heeled waders –
And the soft-curved swans, stepping the mud
To flow across water as smooth as ice.

Beyond here is nothing except the morning,
The salt wind sharp where the sweet flow ends,
And the salmon jostling, thick and bright,
For the journey homeward, the river's birth.

I grew up beside this river;
Its water is my life, tasting
When I fall and bleed
Of the far-off tidings of the sea.